JESUS CARES FOR
WOMEN

HELENE ASHKER

NAVPRESS

Discipleship Inside Out™

Discipleship Inside Out™

NavPress is the publishing ministry of The Navigators, an international Christian organization and leader in personal spiritual development. NavPress is committed to helping people grow spiritually and enjoy lives of meaning and hope through personal and group resources that are biblically rooted, culturally relevant, and highly practical.

For a free catalog go to www.NavPress.com
or call 1.800.366.7788 in the United States or 1.800.839.4769 in Canada.

ISBN-13: 978-0-89109-190-5

All Scripture in this publication is from the *Holy Bible: New International Version®* (NIV®). Copyright © 1973, 1978, 1984 International Bible Society. Used by permission of Zondervan Bible Publishers.

Printed in the United States of America

12 13 14 15 16 / 14 13 12 11

CONTENTS

A U T H O R

Helene Ashker is on full-time staff with The Navigators in Seattle, Washington. She has spent twenty-five years discipling women in the collegiate and community contexts. Helene also speaks at many conferences, counsels, and develops women for leadership.

She attended Brooklyn College and Denver Seminary. She has worked for the *New York Daily News* in the advertising department, but has spent most of her time and energy ministering to women.

ACKNOWLEDGMENTS

I want to express my sincere appreciation to Paula Rinehart and Leslie Holt for the many hours they spent editing this Bible study. "I always thank God for you because of his grace given you in Christ Jesus" (1 Corinthians 1:4).

INTRODUCTION
What makes this Bible study unique?

A woman can have dozens of personal contacts with other women and have all the spiritual insight in the world. *But*—if she doesn't have some friendly, unintimidating means of communicating the good news of Jesus Christ to those women, her spirituality can quickly lose its vitality.

This Bible study offers an opportunity for *any* Christian woman to approach some of those special friends up-close, sharing together in some cozy, non-threatening setting, discussing the lives and problems of some women who happened to live a long time ago. Rather than badgering your friends with cold theology, this study uses a relationship approach, inviting them in with warmth and relevance.

There are two major sections for the woman who is leading the Bible study—the Overview and the Leader's Guide—and then there's a five-part Bible study section in the back. This section is for the women who are coming to discuss what Jesus has to offer them. The Bible study pages are designed without page numbers so that the group leader can make photocopies of each lesson for all the women in her special circle of friends.

This Bible study prepares *you* to be God's representative on your block, in your office, anywhere that He has given you an opportunity to take part in the spiritual harvest.

O V E R V I E W

How to use this Bible study

The quest for fulfillment has been the driving force behind women of the '80s. As women tune into the highly mobile, high-tech society around them, they begin to turn their energies to new frontiers. To excel, to succeed, even to surpass the accomplishments of their male counterparts, has been the goal of many women who have challenged men's domain. Women have emerged in top leadership positions in the corporate boardroom, the military, the sports arena, and academia. Women hold cabinet offices in the government and have won seats in both houses of Congress—even a chair on the Supreme Court.

Now, however, as women examine who they have become, many are wondering where they really belong. It has become painfully clear that achievement and success have not delivered the payoff of personal fulfillment that women have sought. In the brief reflective spaces sandwiched between their frenzied commitments, women are now realizing that external accomplishments do not meet their deepest inner longings. So the search for fulfillment continues.

The desire to find continuity and meaning draws women toward the spiritual arena, where cults are flourishing. As believers, we know that only Jesus can fill the void in these women's lives. What women desperately need today is exposure to vital Christianity.

All of us rub shoulders with a variety of women every day—mothers who trade off car-pooling children, women with whom we share a coffee or lunch break at work, or perhaps a coed in a dorm you study with. Do you ever find yourself wondering, "How could I get to know her in a way where I could share, in a relaxed, easy manner, the possibility of a relationship with Jesus Christ?" Well, this book is written just for you.

I know only too well the feelings of inadequacy that often accompany even the most well-meaning desire to share your faith. For many years when I tried to share what Christ meant to me, my palms got sweaty, every nerve in my body seemed tense. Even the verses I thought I knew disappeared from my memory while I fumbled for the right words. I found myself anxious and confused about the gospel. I prayed for individuals to come to Christ—but when the opportunity arose to actually share something with them about the Lord, I felt paralyzed by inadequacy.

I began to develop friendships with the women in my life. As I took a sincere interest in their lives, listening and appreciating each woman as a person of value, many casual opportunities came my way to share what Jesus Christ means to me. A caring person with a cheerful spirit and a willingness to serve stands out starkly amidst the self-promoting atmosphere of the marketplace or neighborhood.

Though I often failed to consistently show these qualities, the Lord somehow revealed Himself. One woman who worked across the aisle from me invited Jesus into her life two months before I discovered it, though I had been befriending her for over a year. My apprehension gradually decreased as I depended on the Holy Spirit, not myself, to enlighten others with the truth. Another invaluable aid was memorizing an outline and related passages of Scripture that clearly and simply explain the gospel. (You will find this outline in the "Leader's Guide" under the section entitled "Additional Helps for Sharing the Gospel.")

Many Christian women—whether in the home, in the marketplace, in a dorm, or on a military base—share a desire to be equipped to accurately and confidently share their faith. From over 250 church women surveyed, I discovered that:

45% have never led a person to Christ,
52% feel inadequate to explain the gospel,
44% fear rejection or ridicule, and
79% feel guilty for not sharing their faith.

My compelling desire in preparing this manual is to help women who have experienced similar fears and difficulties. My purpose is to see you become better equipped to introduce your friends to the Lord. I have therefore designed this manual to:

1. help you hurdle the obstacles of fear and inadequacy that may be preventing you from reaching out with the good news.
2. clearly define the gospel so that you can share it with confidence.

13

3. provide you with guidelines and helpful materials that will assist you as you guide women through the Bible study *Jesus Cares For Women*. This study is designed to reach the contemporary woman by giving her an intimate glimpse at how Jesus interacted with women nearly two thousand years ago.
4. draw Christian women to a deeper appreciation and identity with Jesus Christ.

You will have an opportunity to invite the women you know to meet Jesus Christ for perhaps the first time. Not only will they see how Jesus related to women, but they will also discover answers to these questions:

Who is Jesus Christ?
Why did He come?
How did He treat women?
How can women know Him today?

As you learn to use this Bible study as an evangelistic tool, you may not see immediate results. But do not be disheartened. God orchestrates the encounters we have with others. It should encourage us when we can be one link in a chain that brings a person to Christ.

Sometimes after praying with a woman to receive Christ, I ask her if anyone in her family is a Christian. Very often a grandmother, aunt, or parent has been praying for her salvation for many years. George Mueller prayed that his brother would receive Christ, but it wasn't until George's funeral that his brother became a believer. I have received letters of appreciation from concerned relatives thanking me for my part. My part may have been very small compared to theirs, but the Lord works out the timetable. We may not know this side of heaven who receives Christ and who does not, but we have fulfilled our mission if the good news is shared.

Women in Jesus' Time: A Brief Historical Overview

To fully appreciate Jesus' approach to women, we need to resist our impulse to approach Scripture from our twentieth-century cultural perspective. Our understanding of Scripture is more accurate if we step back in time—into the shoes of the women of the first century AD.

14

What was it like to be a woman living around the rim of the Mediterranean during Jesus' time? How was a woman's role defined by the cultural and religious constraints of that era? By examining the context in which Jesus presented His radical teaching, we begin to appreciate His extraordinary approach in relating to women.

Imagine a time when a man was commended because he killed his wife for appearing in public without her veil; when a Roman woman's rights were completely subject to her father's power. If she married, then those rights, even the power of life and death, were transferred to her husband. Think of what it would have been like to bear and raise a son who would receive more esteem from his father and the rest of society than you would as his mother.

In both Greek and Roman cultures, women held a second-rate status. Their legal rights were practically nonexistent. In fact, only a husband could petition for a divorce. In such a society, permissive polygamy was considered normal—for men. The owning of multiple wives was an indication of wealth. Needless to say, such a practice only further relegated women to an inferior position since they were treated like property, a mere commodity to indicate status or position.

Jewish women fared only slightly better than their contemporaries in surrounding cultures. A married woman with children did hold a certain place of honor as a wife and mother, but even that position was tied to her ability to produce male children. Because of a twisted interpretation of the Mosaic Law, the rabbinical leaders taught that women were uneducable. They were considered unreliable as courtroom witnesses. Women were even held responsible for the lustful temptations men suffered.

But perhaps the plight of Jewish women could be best summarized by the prayer that the Pharisees were known to regularly pray: "Thank You, God, that I am not a slave, a Gentile, or a woman."

Thus as Jesus' ministry unfolded, the average citizen of Israel began to witness an extraordinary approach to women, one that cut against the grain of commonly held practices. As the radical rabbi, Jesus:

traveled with and was supported by women (Luke
    8:1-3),
spoke to them in public (Mark 5:34),
witnessed to them (John 4:7-26),
gave priority to their education (Luke 10:38-42),
allowed them to honor Him (Mark 14:6-9), and
befriended them (John 11:5).

Jesus treated women as no man had ever treated them before. His warmth, personal attention, tenderness, sound teaching, and compassion toward women was revolutionary. He openly demonstrated His love for each individual He met—both men and women—for whom He would ultimately die.

Partners Together

It is a staggering thing, but it is true—the relationship in which single human beings know God is one in which God, so to speak, takes them on to His staff, to be henceforth His fellow-workers (1 Corinthians 3:9) and personal friends.

J.I. Packer,
Knowing God,
InterVarsity Press

Those of us who are born into the family of God through Jesus Christ not only have the privilege of being His daughters, but are also His representatives. We are Christ's ambassadors—His official messengers. As we move about our home, school, military base, or the marketplace, we represent the Lord. We make the conscious choice to share His message: "For God so loved the world that he gave his one and only Son, that whoever believes in him shall not perish but have eternal life" (John 3:16). Or, as Paul said, God has given us this message: "Be reconciled to God" (2 Corinthians 5:20).

Being an ambassador sometimes means taking risks for Christ. We may have an awkward sense, when sharing Christ, of being uncomfortably vulnerable. What if this woman perceives me as some wild-eyed fanatic?

Actually, though, it is God who has taken the greater

risk. He has authorized and commissioned ordinary, frail individuals like you and me as His own personal staff. Through us, He reaches out to a lost world for whom He died.

As we step out as His ambassadors, we find that our own relationship with the Lord deepens. When we commit ourselves to share the good news in obedience to Him, Jesus works with us and through us. We work not *for* Him but *with* Him. In this dynamic relationship, Jesus carries the responsibility. He provides the opportunities, as well as the courage needed to speak about Him. He gives us the wisdom needed to answer questions—and the ability to admit which questions we are still seeking answers to ourselves. God's commitment to us relieves us of unnecessary pressure and fear. We are in this together.

Reaching the Women in Your Life
One day in church I was introduced by a mutual friend to a beautiful young woman who was the top TV advertising model for her agency that year. By contemporary standards she was quite successful. But as I got to know her, I began to see the other side of that seemingly successful life. As she told me about her broken marriage, her dependency on tranquilizers, and her responsibility for her small children, my heart went out to her. Underneath the veneer of success I could glimpse the miserably empty life this woman lived.

In my living room she described how she had observed a special quality of life in a man who had witnessed to her and in myself, thus arousing her curiosity. When she discovered that God would unconditionally forgive and accept her, she quietly gave her life to Christ. She realized that it was not her own efforts but rather Jesus' substitutionary death for her sins that made her acceptable to God. Through her life, many others have subsequently found the Savior.

There are (as I am sure you realize) many women who live and work around you who are just like the one I have mentioned—women living in quiet desperation. God has called us to a "search and rescue" mission. But that can be hazardous work, can't it?

Have you ever felt the tendency to withdraw from women around you who have habits you disapprove of? Perhaps they use offensive language. Maybe they have lived with a long line of different men. As our culture increasingly becomes a moral wasteland, you and I will encounter more and more women, more and more individuals, whom we would prefer to leave for someone else to reach—unless, that is, we observe and imitate the compassion of Jesus.

Jesus consistently moved toward individuals with deep needs—the promiscuous woman at the well, lepers, the demon-possessed. He differentiated between the sinner and the sin. The love and acceptance people felt in Jesus' presence magnetically drew them to Him.

Our lifestyles, not merely our words, must reflect that we are reaching out in friendship to the lost. When a woman senses that we truly accept her—warts and all—she begins to want to know what makes us different. What I must continually ask myself is, "Does my heart ache for the proud, confused, lonely, or self-sufficient individuals I work with and live near?"

Over half of the church women surveyed indicated that fear of rejection or ridicule often kept them from befriending the lost. It is tough to be laughed at, avoided, or ignored. Yet often those women who appear offended or uninterested are the most vulnerable to the gospel. Courage and compassion come from realizing where they will ultimately spend eternity without Jesus Christ.

Amy Carmichael, missionary to India's mistreated children, portrayed Christians as those who sit in a field picking daisies while a steady stream of people, unreached by the gospel, plummet over a cliff to their deaths. She was criticized by complacent Christians a century ago for being too graphic. Yet the more we allow ourselves to think about the urgent spiritual needs of those who don't know Christ, the more we will move compassionately toward them with the gospel.

Take a moment now to think about all the people you know personally who are not yet believers. Ask yourself, "Who will tell them about Jesus? What must life be like to them now without Him? What will an agonizing eternity be like without hope and without Jesus?" Then ask the Lord for creative opportunities and for courage that overcomes the fear of ridicule.

The Need to Pray

Prayer is the battle, witnessing is taking the spoils.

Lorne Sanny

One secret I have learned over the years is that opportunities to share Christ come in answer to specific prayer. When my prayer life slacks off, opportunities slip by. I begin to miss even the obvious opportunities. Then, in retrospect, I feel guilty. When I am faithful in prayer, however, opportunities arise in unusual ways—whether I am on an airplane with total strangers, or just talking to my neighbors. Often an unbeliever will bring up a need or concern.

You might find it helpful to prepare a list of all family members, friends, and acquaintances who do not yet know the Lord. Consider praying for these people in some of the following ways:

—Intercede regularly, believing God for their salvation.
—Pray for opportunities to serve them, entertain them, or develop a friendship with them.
—Pray for sensitivity in those the Lord is already speaking to.
—Pray for natural ways to share what Jesus means to you.
—Pray for a positive response when you invite them to investigate the Bible to see what Jesus thinks of women.
—Pray for sensitivity to know when they are ready to receive the gift of salvation by faith.
—Thank the Lord for the privilege of representing Him to them.

Pray for Yourself

Though it may seem threatening to discuss spiritual issues with others, someone took that risk with each of us. "Be strong in the Lord and in his mighty power" (Ephesians

6:10). As we commit ourselves to reaching out to those who don't know Christ, divine power flows to us by faith. In response to the Great Commission, we enter the field of battle. Satan hates Jesus Christ and jealously protects his turf. But "the one who is in you is greater than the one who is in the world" (1 John 4:4).

Pray that the Lord will replace the spirit of timidity with courage to speak boldly, just as Paul asked his friends to pray for him: "Pray . . . for me, that whenever I open my mouth, words may be given me so that I will fearlessly make known the mystery of the gospel, for which I am an ambassador in chains. Pray that I may declare it fearlessly, as I should" (Ephesians 6:19-20). If Paul needed prayer for courage, then we are in good company when we ask the Lord for help.

Thinking Practically

Who to invite—As you think of who to invite to do this study with you, I would encourage you to invite women you have already befriended—perhaps someone in your neighborhood, at your job, or at school. You can work on developing a rapport with these women by doing things together of common interest. You might, for example, share a meal together, attend a concert, go shopping, play racquetball, make Christmas ornaments, or go to a museum. Often the most confident, capable women have deep needs. In spite of their prominence or position, they are unable to adequately fill the void inside. They face a hopeless future, whether they know it or not. Without Christ, they have many unanswered questions. As they consider, in this study, who Christ is and how He related to women, they may indeed recognize in Him the fulfillment of their deepest desires.

I like to imagine that this is what the average nonChristian woman would say, if she could, to those of us who know Christ: "Though I may appear self-assured, cold, or disinterested, there is an aching void, an unfulfilled longing in my heart for answers. I am the woman you have known in your neighborhood, at the office, or rooming down the hall from you. I am the one who cries out to belong, to be accepted, to find meaning in life. I may mistakenly think the answer is an impressive job, advanced education, or a husband I can trust, but what I really need is Jesus Christ. You and only a few others I have met seem different, sincere, more caring about people. You are not perfect, but that helps me know that you understand my struggles. Unless I find the answer to life, I am doomed to helplessness, here and for all eternity."

As we spend more time with those we desire to reach, their value system inevitably reveals itself. Through the sensitizing touch of the Holy Spirit, we can identify their vulnerabilities and more readily share how Jesus meets those needs when a person turns to Him.

How to invite someone to this study—You might approach a woman by saying, "Some of us are getting together to investigate what Jesus thinks about women. Would you be interested in joining us?" Or you might ask, "Have you ever wondered what Jesus thinks about women? Some of us. . . ." You may wish to add the following information: "Each chapter we study tells the story of a personal encounter that Jesus had with a woman. We will discover together what He was like—and who He claimed to be. The study will show how what we learn about Jesus and women applies to us today."

How to conduct the study—This study is designed to use one-on-one or in small groups, preferably between four to ten. Nonbelievers should outnumber the believers. Your goal is to help the nonbelievers be comfortable. Encourage the few Christians who bring a nonChristian friend to resist the urge to fill in any lapses of discussion. Allow nonChristians to respond freely—even if you must wait for that response, even if many of their answers seem questionable. Also be sure to affirm their response in some way.

Find a quiet room conducive to easy discussion. A conference room, a dorm room, a private room at the office, or a cozy room at home works well. If you meet at lunch time or over a meal, the leader should eat before or after the discussion, for she will not be able to easily manage eating during the study. Other women may wish to bring a brown bag lunch.

Consider using an icebreaker question the first week,

such as, "What did you, as a child, want to be when you grew up?" "What is your favorite room in your home, and why?" "What flower do you think best describes you?" "What famous woman in history do you admire most?"

Each chapter can be covered adequately in an hour or less. Be sure to stop on time, not allowing the study to drag on. You can use an additional meeting if the material is not adequately covered.

The person guiding each session may study the "Leader's Guide" for additional material on each chapter in preparation for the meeting. The most helpful outside study is careful reading and meditation on each of the five New Testament scenes.

Provide Bibles for each person attending. The same translation is preferable. Perhaps your church has Bibles you could borrow. The Gideons and the American Bible Society both sell Bibles at a reasonable price, which can be used for group study.

We recommend that you reproduce and hand out a copy of the Bible study chapter to each woman when she arrives. Give out only one chapter at a time. Let the women know that they may write on and keep their copies.

This study is designed to be done together so that there is no need to assign homework. Everyone can jot down answers as the study progresses. Or, after reading each scene, you may want to provide five minutes for everyone to look over the questions and jot down whatever answers come to mind. Some of the women will then feel more prepared to discuss.

Use a discussion format. Do not teach the lesson. Personal discovery and sharing verbally is a far more effective learning technique than passive listening. Most people enjoy contributing to the discussion. Furthermore, they tend to remember longer what they discover for themselves.

The atmosphere and interaction of a group of non-Christians investigating the Bible will not be like that of the average Christian Bible study group you may be more familiar with. For many of these nonbelievers, this will probably be the first time they have seriously opened a Bible in years, if at all. While they may feel comfortable with psychology

22

books or income tax forms, the Bible is a new book, which presents the distinct possibility of exposing their ignorance.

So, as the leader, you need to be prepared to wade through longer pauses in the flow of responses. What seems like an obvious answer to you will require time and contemplation for a person who is unfamiliar with the Bible.

Allow the women to ask questions aimed at further clarification or insight. In fact, you may want to ask at some point each week, "What other questions does this passage bring to your mind?" In preparation, you may also fill in with additional questions.

As You Begin

Relax, and you will help them relax. Have each woman give her name and tell a little about herself. Follow with an icebreaker question.

Explain that the reason you are meeting is to discover what Jesus thinks about women and also the essence of Christianity—who Jesus is and what He did for us. The Bible will be the primary reference book.

Hand out materials: Bibles, pens, and a copy of the first chapter of the study to each person. Remind the women that the copy is theirs to write on and keep.

You might start out by reading the introductory story out loud, with them following along in their own copy. Then someone in the group can read the Bible passage aloud with the rest following along. To assist them in locating the passage, you might show them where the book is located in the Bible, or if everyone has the same translation, you can give the page number. You may also give them a few minutes to reread the passage of Scripture silently after it has been read aloud, giving them more opportunity to assimilate the story. They should try to have the scene clearly pictured in their minds. Help them envision the drama, and feel the tension and emotions. Before you start right into the questions that follow, it helps to casually talk through the scene as a group. For example: "Where is this scene taking place? Who are the main characters?"

The biblical scene and passage is familiar to us as Christians. But if the scene remains unclear and otherworldly for the nonChristian (just like some remote passage from Shakespeare), she won't be able to respond to the questions you want to discuss later about the passage.

Suggestions for Better Group Dynamics

Some women may feel they should answer every question. If one person seems to dominate, it often helps to smile and suggest that someone else answer.

Conversely, if your questions are answered by silence, you may need to gently ask one of the women by name, "What do you think, Alice?"

The women in your study have a variety of backgrounds and personalities—all of which affects the atmosphere of your study. Occasionally you will encounter someone with an argumentative spirit, which can create an uncomfortable situation. Remember, a soft answer still turns away wrath. We do not have to defend Scripture, but only to graciously present Jesus as the Bible reveals Him.

Be careful not to be drawn away from the study content and discuss unrelated or controversial issues, such as the role of women in the church or the marketplace. Make every effort to keep your group centered on the person and work of Jesus Christ and how *He* related to women.

If after one or two sessions some women in your group drop out, do not be discouraged. Continue on, encouraged with those who come. Sharing the gospel with just one person is adequate reason to continue any study.

One thing I discovered in piloting this study is that unbelievers who finish it, though not ready to make a decision, are often open to continue studying the Bible. Here are some suggestions for material for continued study:

Studies in Christian Living (NavPress)

The study of John in Appendix of *Living Proof* by Jim Petersen (NavPress)

Her Name Is Woman by Gien Karssen (NavPress)

Many women have so little knowledge that they need more time to study Christ and His message. I would suggest that any further study would continue to return to the basic issues of the gospel.

Becoming Fruitful by Being Faithful

That which must reach the heart must come from the heart.
Anonymous

The highest honor Jesus offered His disciples was His friendship (John 15:13-15). Jesus had every right to call us servants or slaves, for He bought us with His precious blood. But He called us into companionship or fellowship because He has such a great love and commitment toward us (1 Corinthians 1:9).

Often in sharing our faith, we give the *plan* of salvation. Far more effective and appealing is sharing about the *Person* who saves . . . introducing one Friend to another friend. The more intimate we are with Jesus Christ, the more intimately we can share Him with another.

Are you spending consistent time with Jesus so that you can develop your relationship with Him? A recent national survey indicated that only four percent of believing Christians spend personal time alone with the Lord in reading the Bible and in prayer on a daily basis. Could we be missing the opportunity to introduce women to Jesus because we are not growing in our own walk with Him?

With all the demands to excel that bombard today's woman, it is sometimes difficult to give our personal relationship with the Lord the highest priority. Most of us are caught in an impossible balancing act of trying to assume responsibilities in the home, the church, and the marketplace. Many are thoroughly exhausted trying to do it all. Sadly, the One who could give us wisdom and rest as we labor is neglected.

Jesus told Martha that she was worried and upset about many things. Only one thing was really needed, He said, and that was to sit at His feet as Mary, her sister, had done. Mary had chosen to sit at Jesus' feet—listening, learning, and loving (Luke 10:41-42).

It is imperative that our relationship with Jesus increasingly becomes our highest priority as we seek to reach out to those who don't know Christ. A fresh word of comfort, direction, or instruction from the Lord reflects on our faces and in our attitudes. As the sweetness of Jesus permeates our lives, all those in our sphere of influence will smell His perfume. Though they may sometimes react negatively, they cannot deny the scent that drew us to know Jesus Christ (2 Corinthians 2:14-16). We are now the channels through whom Jesus has chosen to reveal Himself—what a blessed privilege.

Let us not mistakenly leave evangelism to those we perceive have the "gift of evangelism." God can reveal Himself through any available, willing person. You have fulfilled your responsibility as a member of God's staff if you befriend a woman, do any or all of this study with her, give your testimony, help her understand who Jesus is and why He came, and, when possible, give her the opportunity to invite Jesus into her life.

"You are my witnesses," declares the LORD, "and my servant whom I have chosen."

Isaiah 43:10

LEADER'S GUIDE

Helps for leading this study

As we now move to the actual study, perhaps a little synopsis of people's need for the gospel will be helpful. Ultimately, as you conduct this study, it should be your objective to help women discover who Jesus is, why He came, and what He thinks of women. Let's examine these issues.

Why Jesus Came

God originally created man and woman as perfect beings with a personal freedom of choice. Each was made in the image of God—able to think, feel, and choose. Equal in value, together they reflected the image of God (Genesis 1:27). God further honored them by giving them daily companionship and communion with Himself. They brought great joy to the heart of God as they fellowshiped together. This was God's original loving plan: that mankind would live in perfect harmony, enjoying His full acceptance and love.

Tragically, by wrongfully exercising their God-given freedom of choice, this man and woman succumbed to Satan's lies rather than believing God. Everything changed from that moment on—for them and for us. Because of deliberate disobedience, the intimate relationship they had with God was severed. No longer could they walk in harmony and be fully identified with Him. Without God's companionship, their identity and unity with God and each other degenerated from perfect concord into discord. Paradise was lost.

God had warned the man and the woman: "You are free to eat from any tree in the garden; but you must not eat from the tree of the knowledge of good and evil, for when you eat of it you will surely die" (Genesis 2:16-17). God, therefore, could have rightfully abandoned the man and woman—and all of us as well—to a hopeless eternity in hell. Though man's love for God had been marred by rebellion, independence, and pride, God's love for man has not changed.

There was only one way man could be forgiven and reconciled to God. God Himself had to take the death penalty due man. *This is the focal point of this study: How God, in love, provided a Substitute so that His alienated creation could be forgiven and invited to full reconciliation with Him.*

When God's original plan for man was thwarted, not only was man justly cursed, but so was all of creation. The catastrophes we experience—wars, murders, earthquakes, sickness, and ultimately death—are the consequences of man's rebellion against God (Romans 8:20-22).

This preceding thumbnail sketch of human history should be helpful if you are asked these questions: Why does God allow disease, disaster, and death? And, more importantly, why do we desperately need a *Savior*?

Brief Overview of This Study

You will notice that the first two chapters of *Jesus Cares For Women* introduce you to Jesus as a gracious, compassionate champion of women. Observe Him entering into their pain and sorrow. Watch Him as He lovingly meets each woman's needs. The third, fourth, and fifth chapters attempt to further reveal who Jesus is, and why He came. By examining how Jesus responded to the last three women in this study, we see Jesus' willingness to forgive our sin, His substitutionary death for us, and the hope that His resurrection gives us for eternal life with Him. In this leader's guide, we will take a look at what you, as a group leader, should emphasize, highlighting key questions and sections in each chapter.

CHAPTER ONE

The major emphasis of Chapter 1 is the power and compassion Jesus demonstrates as He relates to others.

Many people view God as an impersonal force, not in touch or involved with our pain, fears, and needs. But when the people see Jesus bring the young man back to life, they exclaim, "God has come to help his people."

Jesus personally invites us to bring our deepest longings, heartaches, and anxieties to Him today, just as men and women did then. Jesus never changes. "[He] is the same yesterday and today and forever" (Hebrews 13:8).

29

Considering Christ Section

To illustrate His point in Matthew 11:28-30, Jesus uses the yoke, which was a familiar item in the Jewish culture. A yoke is a wooden bar placed over the shoulders of two oxen, who thus share the weight of the burden together. When we are "yoked" with Jesus as we bring our needs to Him, our end of the weight is light.

A good question for believers to consider, as well as those who are seeking Jesus, is this: "What does it mean to truly bring my deepest concerns to Jesus? Have I done that?" When I do bring my needs to Him by faith, the weight of my concerns falls on Him. And although He may not entirely remove the burden, He will surely lighten my end of the load as I cast my cares upon Him.

The implication in this passage is that we are to come and keep coming to Jesus to have our needs met. Learning this basic step of faith will help women identify what God is like: His power extends over even life and death. He is loving, constantly reaching out to meet needs, sometimes before we've even asked.

CHAPTER TWO

The major emphasis of Chapter 2 is that Jesus is God, and that He honors an individual's faith in Him.

In the previous chapter, Jesus dramatically displays His power over life and death. In this section, He demonstrates His power over physical illness. Because He sees this woman's need, He does not pass her by. He seems acutely aware of her pain, and so He reaches out to help. In addition to aiding the harassed and helpless, Jesus verifies that He is not only sent by God, but that in fact He *is* God.

There were many false teachers then, just as there are today, claiming either to represent God or to be divine. Even the Lord Jesus' disciples ask Him, "Show us the Father." In John 14:6, Jesus emphatically states that He is the only way to God. Being sincere or doing good works, though commendable, will not bring anyone to God. Jesus is the only way.

Questions 3 and 5:
Questions 3 and 5 are related in that the woman's determination stemmed from her desperation and provided the courage to risk the dangers of a pressing crowd. Her faith was no doubt based on what she had heard from others about Jesus (Matthew 14:35-36).

Question 4:
When looking at this question, it may be important for you to note that Jesus knew that the people ostracized this woman from society because of her physical malady. Since no one knew who was healed and there was no outward evidence of healing, this woman faced the problem of convincing people that she was no longer an outcast. To help her, Jesus not only healed her, but He publicly confirmed her healing so that she would be reinstated into community life.

All through the Gospels, Jesus honored an individual's faith in Him. He also made a point of rebuking His disciples and others for their lack of faith. Jesus took the time to point out to both the men and women in the crowd that this woman's faith was the reason for her healing.

Although a far more impressive male leader had asked Jesus to come to his home to heal his daughter (Mark 5:22-24), Jesus stopped the whole procession to talk to this poor, outcast woman as though she were the only one there. God's love knows no partiality (Ephesians 6:9, James 3:17). More importantly, Jesus said, "Daughter, your faith has healed you. Go in peace." This comforting statement denotes a sense of wholeness: He had put her life back together. By addressing her as "daughter," He indicated that she was now entering into a new relationship with Him. Jesus honored her faith, which met not only her physical and social needs, but also her spiritual needs.

Question 5:
There are several possible answers to this question.

(a) The woman may have felt that in coming up behind Jesus that she was healed without His consent. Jesus reassured her that what she had done was very acceptable.

(b) She might have feared that she would anger this "Rabbi." Touching Jesus made Him, technically speaking, ceremonially unclean—her particular physical problem rendered anyone unclean who touched her (Leviticus 15:19-20). It is important to let the women in your group know that men with a similar problem were also considered unclean, so that the Old Testament requirements do not seem preferential to men (Leviticus 15:4-6). One reason Old Testament rules of cleanliness were given by God was to protect the people from communicable diseases. The connection between germs and disease was not discovered until centuries later.

Considering Christ Section
The crucial issue that divides believers from unbelievers is "Who is Jesus Christ?" Many consider Him to be only a great teacher or prophet. But until someone acknowledges His deity—that Jesus Christ is the Son of God who has come in the flesh, fully God and fully man—that person cannot truly know Him (1 John 4:1-3). In Matthew 16:13-17, Jesus commends Peter for the accuracy of his answer, indicating that only Jesus' Father could have revealed this to Peter.

CHAPTER THREE

The major emphasis of Chapter 3 is that Jesus came to forgive us of our sins.

In the previous two chapters we see Jesus reaching out to meet the deep emotional and physical pain of two women. This third chapter begins to plumb the depths of the spiritual need that all of us have in common. Jesus' gracious concern for the rejected woman in this chapter is obvious.

For these religious leaders to rudely humiliate this woman because of her adulterous act only further demonstrates the sinfulness of those who are accusing her. As Romans 3:23 states, we are all sinners. Those who come to judge this woman's sin end up leaving embarrassingly aware of their own. They set out to trick Jesus but depart in defeat—convicted by their own guilty consciences.

Through this woman, Jesus reveals why He came: "God did not send his Son into the world to condemn the world, but to save the world through him" (John 3:17). Jesus does not gloss over this woman's offense. As God, He chooses to forgive her. By lovingly forgiving this woman, Jesus protects her—yet without challenging the Roman law or defying the Old Testament Law. God's ways and thoughts truly are higher than ours, as Jesus' teaching brilliantly exemplifies.

Question 2:
If the Pharisees had been so interested in keeping the Law, they would have also brought the adulterous man to Jesus (Leviticus 20:10). Jesus saw through their motives, and protected the woman from being unfairly singled out.

Question 4:
Jesus Christ was the only one qualified to stone her because He is the only one without sin. However, His desire was and always is to rescue rather than to condemn (John 3:16-19).

Question 7:
Instead of slipping away with the crowd, the guilty woman remained, her eyes riveted on Jesus. No man had ever respected and valued her like this man. Never had she seen a face so righteous, and yet so accepting.

Questions 8 and 9:
By pointing out in John 3:16-17 that God's motive in sending Jesus was love—to rescue rather than condemn—you will be introducing the gospel on a very positive note. In the next chapter, the women will see that God could rescue us because Jesus willingly submitted Himself to the excruciating crucifixion. He is our Substitute, having experienced the death we each deserve.

To condemn means to pass sentence upon someone. Thus to be forgiven means that this woman's debts have been completely cancelled. What should be emphasized here is that God desires to forgive us in spite of our willful rebellion. Underscoring these points in your discussion of Chapter 3 will set the stage for the presentation in Chapter 4 of why Jesus died.

Promiscuity is so common in our modern society that it is essential to point out that the Bible nevertheless calls such behavior sin. But Jesus is just as willing to forgive us today as He was then (John 8:23-24). We all stand guilty of willful disobedience before God. Neither the woman nor the crowd of men denied their guilt before the penetrating gaze of Jesus Christ. Instead of acknowledging their guilt, however, the men slunk away. The woman stayed and willingly received the pardon Jesus offered. She obviously must have believed in Him, and therefore she was forgiven.

Question 10:
Jesus referred to the issue of repentance in His last words to this woman: "Go now and leave your life of sin."

> *Repentance:* In the New Testament the subject chiefly has reference to repentance from sin, and this change of mind involves both a turning from sin and a turning to God.
>
> W. E. Vine,
> *Vine's Expository Dictionary of New Testament Words,*
> Revell, page 281

All God's directives and restrictions are ultimately for provision and protection. Sin has broken our relationship with our holy, wise, and sovereign God. Sin also hinders our relationships with each other. Eventually it has the power to destroy us as well.

Considering Christ Section
This story clearly indicates that we all stand guilty before a holy God. Many people today are willing to admit they are not perfect. But only by acknowledging our sin to Jesus, as this woman must have done in His presence, can we receive forgiveness. She was dragged into His presence but remained there voluntarily and received His gracious pardon.

When Adam and Eve chose to disregard God's instructions, they experienced the consequences of rebellion: exile from God's presence. As the offspring of Adam and Eve, every one of us is born with a rebellious or sinful nature. Therefore, we are born already separated from God.

It is commonly thought that God is everyone's Father. In truth, however, God is everyone's Creator. He *will be* everyone's Father only as people are reborn spiritually into the family of God. The human birth that we were given is only a prelude to being born again spiritually into God's family. Each of us must come to Jesus, acknowledging our rebelliousness and accepting His forgiveness.

CHAPTER FOUR

The major emphasis of Chapter 4 is that Jesus paid the penalty for our sin.

In the previous chapter, the women in your study met the Savior as He intervenes on behalf of a woman who is on the verge of being stoned to death for her sin. Here Jesus compassionately demonstrates His forgiveness of even the most serious of social offenses.

Now, in Chapter 4, we have the opportunity to observe Jesus' willingness to come as the sacrifice that God required— to pay the penalty for all of us, for we have fallen short of His standards. The gospel message, introduced in Chapter 3 with John 3:16-17, continues to be revealed in Chapter 4. God in His love, sent Jesus to live among us and to reveal what He is like. Now in this scene we want to highlight the death of Jesus Christ.

Question 1:
Jesus personally befriended women. Mary was one of the women with whom He had a long-term friendship.

Question 2:
Mary was perhaps the only one present who grasped the significance of the event that was about to take place in Jerusalem. She was anointing the body of Jesus with costly perfume. Nard, or spikenard, is a fragrant oil obtained from

35

an East Indian plant. In Jesus' day, it was imported from India in special alabaster jars, which were carefully sealed to conserve the perfume. At that time imported goods were extremely expensive.

Question 3:
In the marketplace of the 1980s, "over a year's wages" could average easily $15,000 to $20,000. The money spent on the nard could have been her dowry.

Question 4:
Jesus understood Mary's intentions. First, He defended her, and then He said, "She has done a beautiful thing to me." He goes on to give her a personal memorial. Mary's story is recorded in three of the four Gospels.

Considering Christ Section
It is important to help others realize that the death of Christ is the central drama of Scripture. From the beginning (Genesis 3:15) to the end (Revelation 5:12), the Bible speaks of the saving work of Jesus Christ.

Considering these three short sections of Scripture will give you the opportunity to demonstrate the importance of the death of Christ. Notice how clearly Isaiah states that Christ was bruised for *our* iniquities and sins. Isaiah 53:6 is one of the Bible's clearest explanations of sin: to go our own way.

In John 10, Jesus expressly speaks of laying down His life for His sheep. And finally, the verses in Colossians allude to the Roman custom of nailing an announcement of a criminal's offenses to the cross on which he would die. Paul's analogy here is that *our* sins, our debt, was nailed to the cross on which Christ died.

Preparing Your Testimony
It would be very appropriate for you (or another Christian in the group) to give a brief personal testimony of how you came to know Christ. You should prepare and practice giving your testimony prior to the session. Perhaps the following guidelines will help you.

During the study time for Chapter 4, you might introduce the use of someone's testimony when you sense the time is appropriate. It is essential that the testimony be very brief, casual, and specific. Simply explain:
  (1) what your life was like before knowing Jesus, stressing one major need that you had (fear, loneliness, searching, or confusion);
  (2) the circumstances surrounding your encounter with Christ, perhaps illustrated with a meaningful verse; and
  (3) the difference Jesus made and continues to make in your life.
Avoid superlatives that may indicate that your life has no difficulties now. Be honest and realistic so that you will be believable.

Many cults today use personal testimonies as a means of winning converts, but with the help of the Holy Spirit, our testimonies have the unique ring of truth. Take precaution against getting caught up with details that are unimportant to the listener. If your intention is to honor Jesus, we can trust the Holy Spirit to bring the listeners under conviction of sin and to lift the veil from their blinded eyes.

A Courtroom Scene
It is often helpful to use an analogy so that unbelievers can understand the substitutionary death of Christ. Almost everyone can imagine a contemporary courtroom scene. Here is an example of how you might share this aspect of Christ's death with another person:

"Suppose you (or I, for that matter) are caught speeding, 60 mph in a 35 mph residential zone. The policeman pulls you over to the side of the road and confronts you with his radar reading. He then gives you a speeding ticket and summons you to appear in court.

"Your day in court arrives. You stand before the judge. After reading the charges against you, the judge then bangs his gavel and declares you guilty as charged. He hands you an impossible fine.

"Then, as everyone looks on in amazement, your defense attorney excuses himself from your side, leaves the courtroom, and goes to the clerk's office. He proceeds to write out his personal check to pay *your* fine. The clerk stamps the check: 'Debt paid in full.' The case is closed. You are dismissed from paying the fine because the debt was paid for you.

"Similarly, each of us stands guilty before God (our heavenly Judge). Because we have broken His laws, we are faced with His just penalty: death. But our defense attorney, Jesus Christ, volunteers to pay our penalty to die in our place. Because of His substitutionary death, the debt for our sin is 'paid in full.' Our case before God is closed and we are set free because Jesus has purchased our freedom."

CHAPTER FIVE

The two major emphases of Chapter 5 are (1) the significance of the resurrection of Jesus Christ and (2) a clear presentation of the gospel.

The resurrection of Jesus Christ is the pivotal point of the gospel. If Jesus had not risen from the dead, then our hope of seeing Him, as Mary did, or of living beyond the grave would be inconceivable. Christ's resurrection verified God's acceptance of the completed work of the Cross.

The uniqueness of Christianity rests upon the silent witness of an empty tomb. In all other religions, man works to reach "god" by his own effort. Only in Christianity does God take the loving initiative to reconcile men and women to Himself. As you prepare to highlight the great truths of Jesus' resurrection for today's searching woman, meditate on 1 Corinthians 15. This passage will help clarify why His resurrection was essential to our rescue.

Question 1:
Explore how Mary might have felt during the triumphal entry, hearing of Jesus' capture, trial, and execution. Then examine her consternation upon discovering that the tomb was empty when she took her spices to anoint Him. Most women can identify with being emotionally drained in such a situation.

Question 3:
Mary's eyes were no doubt swollen from mourning. Perhaps she did not look up, assuming that the person who stood there was merely a groundskeeper or a soldier. Or, it is possible that Jesus did not reveal Himself to her—in the same way that He hid His identity from the two men on the road to Emmaus. Finally, you might explore her emotions at hearing her name from the lips of her beloved Lord.

Question 4:
Remember that a woman's testimony was not considered valid in the Jewish culture. Yet Jesus trusted her to go to His disciples with the news that He was alive!

Question 5:
Since Peter and John had seen the empty tomb, but not the angels or the Lord, we must conclude that Jesus chose to reveal Himself to Mary first. Though Jesus had already taught that He would die and be resurrected, neither Mary nor His disciples understood this truth until He appeared to them personally.

Question 6:
If Jesus had not risen from the grave, it would have indicated that He was a mere man. Without Christ's resurrection, not one of us would have the hope of eternal life.

Taking the Gospel record as faithful history, there can be no doubt that Christ Himself anticipated His death and resurrection, and plainly declared it to His disciples. . . . The Gospel writers are quite frank to admit that such predictions really did not penetrate their minds till the resurrection was a fact (John 20:9). But evidence is there from the mouth of our Lord that He would come back from the dead after three days. He told them that He would be put to death violently, through the cause of hatred, and would rise the third day. All this came to pass.

Bernard Ramm,
Protestant Christian Evidences,
Moody Press, 1953

Helping Women See Their Need to Receive Jesus

No woman in the New Testament who encountered Jesus ever turned down His invitation. The uniqueness of Christ's love stirred women's hearts to respond to Him. As you complete your time with the women in this study, you have the privilege of helping them come to a place of actively responding to Jesus by accepting His gift of eternal life for themselves.

At this point, it is important for the women to realize that it is not enough to simply know about Jesus, although that is an important first step. To illustrate the limitation of mere knowledge, you might ask a woman if she knows George Washington. Most likely she will reply that indeed she knows about this famous man. Then you could ask if George Washington knows her. The response you receive will help to demonstrate that having a personal relationship with someone is not accomplished merely by knowing a lot about that individual.

Additional Helps for Sharing the Gospel

You might begin this section by saying, "To be sure that we understand why Jesus came and why Mary was honored, let's summarize the essential points of what we have learned." As you then discuss the gospel, highlight the following major points:

1. God loves us all (John 3:16).
2. All have sinned (Romans 3:23).
3. There is a penalty for sin (Romans 6:23).
4. The penalty was paid by Christ (Romans 5:8).
5. We must receive salvation as a gift (Ephesians 2:8-9).
6. We can have assurance of eternal life (1 John 5:11-13).
7. Why do people resist accepting Jesus? (John 3:18-19).

You can memorize these passages to help familiarize yourself with them so that they are available to be used whenever the Lord gives an opportunity to witness. It would be helpful to memorize the Scripture reference along with the text to enable you to find the verses quickly in your Bible.

Our responsibility is to share the truth and give the

listener the opportunity to make a decision for Christ. God'
part is to draw people lovingly to the point of faith. Whethe
or not the women in your study make an immediate deci
sion, you can rest in the fact that you have obediently don‹
your part. Some women may want time to think about th‹
gospel. You are encouraged to intercede for them in praye
as the Holy Spirit confirms the truth of the Word in thei
lives. Thank the Lord for the privilege of representing Him
and continue to develop your relationships with the womei.
as time goes on.

Sometimes you will delightfully discover that some
women have put their faith in Christ during the period of
time they have been in the study. These new believers, and
perhaps some of the others, may be willing to continue in
Bible study with you. You may wish to lead the *Studies in
Christian Living* series (NavPress) or another appropriate
series to help familiarize your group with Jesus' life and
ministry on a broader scope. Consider assigning some
homework in preparation for your next study now that the
women are more familiar with the Bible.

How to Further Assist a Decision for Christ

As you summarize what has been learned in the study,
review with the women what we have learned: Jesus cares
about meeting our emotional, physical, social, mental, and
spiritual needs. As we have observed through the study,
each woman who encountered Jesus Christ was radically
transformed by His love.

This transforming Christ is still the same today as He
was 2000 years ago. He never changes. He still yearns to
meet the needs of women in our generation. You can
explain to the women in your group that if they were to
come to Christ as women have from the first century on, He
would:

assure them of His love,
forgive their sins,
guide them through life, and
assure them of life with Him forever.

At this point, you might ask the women where they are
in their spiritual pilgrimage: "Do you have any questions

about how you can receive the gift of life Jesus offers?" "Would you like to consider receiving Jesus Christ right now? I would love to help you." Or you might ask, "If you were standing at a friend's deathbed and she wanted to know how to know God, what have you learned that could help her?"

You could pray with women who are ready to commit their lives to Christ. For example, you might ask them to pray, "Lord Jesus, I know that I am a sinner. Thank You for dying on the Cross for my sins. I am asking You to come into my life and make me what You desire. Thank You for coming into my life."

Now that you have brought an unbeliever as far as she was willing to go in this study, thank the Lord for the beautiful feet He is giving you. "How beautiful are the feet of those who bring good news!" (Romans 10:15).

After the five studies are completed, you or whoever invited each woman to the study might set up a time to have coffee or lunch with the individual women in your study. Then you can ask natural questions, such as, "What did you think of the study? Did you have any new thoughts? Have you come to a point of placing your trust in Christ?"

Whether or not those you study with complete the study or receive Christ, you have done what Christ asks us to do by extending the gospel to those in your range of friends and acquaintances. Bravo! You have hurdled several of the barriers many Christians never even attempt. Let me encourage you to continue praying for those on your list, and, along with other Christian friends, to start another group with the *Jesus Cares For Women* study.

Spiritual Pediatrics

Once a woman has committed her life to Jesus Christ, she will need guidance to grow in her newfound faith. Just as a baby needs loving care and nourishing food, so a newborn Christian needs spiritual pediatrics. Suggesting that a new Christian memorize 1 John 5:11-12 will help her base her decision on facts of Scripture (the promises of God) rather than an emotional experience. Continuing to study the Bible with you or other young Christians will help her establish a vibrant relationship with the Lord.

The Navigators have excellent follow-up materials available. For example:

Scripture Memory:

Beginning with Christ

Going On with Christ

Topical Memory System

Topical Memory System: Life Issues

Bible Study Series:

Studies in Christian Living

Design for Discipleship

These series are designed to help young Christians grow spiritually as they learn to apply personally the truths they study.

BIBLE STUDY

How Jesus interacted with five different women

1

The Sorrowing Woman

The two crowds met on the steep slope of a hill near the gates of the city of Nain. They were located six miles from Jesus' hometown of Nazareth. The view was wide across the plains. They could see the snowy heights of Mount Hermon on the horizon.

Jesus and a large number of His disciples climbed up the hill, as the other group moved down the hill toward the rock-hewn tombs that lined the eastern side of the road. This last group was led by mourners whose shrieks and lamentations pierced the air.

In the middle of the procession, relatives and friends moved slowly under the weight of a young man on an open bier. The dead man's mother walked beside the stretcher, weeping. She was a widow, and now she had lost her only son.

The birth of this son had been an occasion for great celebration. In the Jewish culture, giving birth to a son gave a woman value in her husband's eyes. A baby boy ensured the hope of passing on the family wealth and name. His presence was guaranteed social security. It would be his responsibility to care for his aging parents, and especially for his widowed mother.

It was thus the hope of every Jewish woman to have a son, and God had granted this woman that desire. But now . . . she was left utterly alone. Already she had suffered her husband's death, and now her only son's. She knew, as did those who followed her to the burial caves, that the future held only the grim prospect of destitute dependence upon the mercy of friends and strangers.

As the widow and the procession of mourners were leaving the city gate, just then Jesus and His disciples reached the top of the hill and the city's entrance. Totally of His own initiative, Jesus came alongside to talk to her.

What happened next astounded the widow and the crowd that followed her. No one would have believed it if they hadn't observed the incident with their own eyes. In fact, news of it spread like wildfire through the entire region. People whispered to each other in fearful and awed tones. Soon there wasn't a household in the district that wasn't discussing Jesus and what He had done.

Read Luke 7:11-17 and consider these questions as you discover the conclusion to this story.

Discussion Questions

1. Read Luke 7:12-13 again. Try to imagine what the widow might have been feeling.

2. What motivated Jesus to approach the widow? (verse 13).

3. In this scene, what action did Jesus take? (verses 14-15).

4. If you had been the widow, how would you have responded to what Jesus said and did?

5. What was the crowd's response to this miracle? (verse 16).

6. Judging from what you have seen in this encounter, how would you describe Christ? What kind of person is He?

7. Have you ever had a loss or disappointment so shattering that you felt you wouldn't recover?

Considering Christ

Jesus saw this woman's need and compassionately reached out to help her. He seemed acutely aware of her pain and more than willing to help.

Here is another short, perhaps familiar passage from Matthew's Gospel in which Jesus Himself states His willingness to lift our load. What does Christ promise to give those who carry heavy burdens?

"Come to me, all you who are weary and burdened, and I will give you rest. Take my yoke upon you and learn from me, for I am gentle and humble in heart, and you will find rest for your souls. For my yoke is easy and my burden is light."

Matthew 11:28-30

He said, "Surely they are my people . . ."; and so he became their Savior. In all their distress he too was distressed.

Isaiah 63:8-9

2

The Suffering Woman

The suffering woman lived in the city of Capernaum, near the harp-shaped Sea of Galilee. She is commonly referred to as "the woman with the issue of blood."

Here was her plight: For twelve long years, this woman had been steadily losing blood. She must have been a woman of some means—at least she possessed enough financial resources to continue to seek out one doctor after another. But the medical world had no more to offer her than if she had lived four hundred years earlier. She may have taken ground-up willow bark to try to reduce her pain. This was a bitter tasting remedy containing salicin, an aspirin-like drug that would have only aggravated her bleeding.

Yet even worse than her physical condition was the social and religious ostracism she was certain to have faced. The prevailing opinions of her day were much the same as our own: Bad things don't happen to good people. You get what you justly deserve. Thus, to be stricken with a chronic, incurable disease such as this was tantamount to a confession of sinful behavior, presumably illicit immorality.

The Old Testament regulation regarding her disease indicated that she was ceremonially unclean and unable to participate in the social and religious life of the Jewish community. She could well have been divorced by her husband and shut off from her family. She was a social and spiritual leper.

She had, no doubt, heard of Jesus and the amazing things He had done. Sometime earlier, in the very same town, Jesus had healed a paralyzed man. He had also spoken some startling words as He healed him: "Son, your sins are forgiven." Of all the audacity! Why, no one could forgive sins but God alone!

Now she heard that Jesus was back in Capernaum. As usual there was a crowd of people around Him, but she was desperate. She had to get to this man. Keeping her face down to avoid being recognized, she waded out into the sweating mass of people following Him. Persistently, she worked her way deeper into the tight circle surrounding Him until finally she was near enough to touch Him. She reached out and lightly touched His garment for just as instant.

In the next moment, an incredible series of events was set into motion. Read Mark 5:21-34 to find out the interesting end to this story. Consider the following questions.

Discussion Questions

1. What motivated this woman to come to Jesus?

2. What emotions do you think this woman experienced as she reached out to touch Jesus?

3. What gave her the determination and strength to push through the close-packed crowd? (Mark 5:34).

4. Why do you think Jesus insisted on publicly identifying this woman?

5. Why was this woman so afraid when she was forced to admit that she was the one who had touched Him?

6. In what ways did Jesus show that He thought of her as a worthwhile individual?

7. What do you think this woman told her family and friends about Jesus when she went home?

8. How do you think Jesus touches lives today?

Considering Christ
This woman was not the only one who came to Christ with a sense that in His identity lay the essence of far more than a mere man. Read Matthew 16:13-17 and note the different speculations that existed concerning who Jesus was. What did He say about Peter's declaration?

Who do people say He is today?

Who does Jesus claim He is? (John 14:8-11).

> *Jesus answered, "Anyone who has seen me has seen the Father."*
>
> John 14:9

3
The Adulterous Woman

At the height of Christ's ministry, the people followed Him everywhere He went. His popularity, however, was an increasing threat to the Jewish leaders. They searched for a way to discredit Him. The woman who is the subject of this study presented the golden opportunity to do so—or so they thought.

On this particular occasion, Jesus appeared in the Temple courts at dawn. There was still a chill in the air, and the sky was streaked with red. People gathered around Him, and soon He sat down and began to teach.

Suddenly angry voices interrupted His lesson. The scribes and the Pharisees (the Jewish religious leaders) elbowed their way to the front like a vigilante squad, dragging a disheveled woman with them.

Shoving her in front of Jesus, they shouted out her sin for all to hear. "Teacher," they said, "this woman was caught in the act of adultery. In the Law Moses commanded us to stone such women. Now what do you say?"

Here, then, was the trap they had waited for, and this woman was merely the bait. If Jesus said to let her go, then He would be guilty of rejecting the Old Testament Law. If He told the scribes and Pharisees to stone her, then the crowd would claim He was no longer a sympathetic friend of common people. He would also be challenging Roman law, which did not allow the Jews to carry out the death sentence.

As this woman stood in front of Jesus with the hostile crowd behind her, she must have been terrified. Death by stoning was painful and prolonged, and that ordeal might well be hers within the hour.

She watched Jesus bend down from where He sat and begin tracing something on the ground in front of her. The accusing voices grew louder and more insistent. At last Jesus straightened up, looked directly at the men, and spoke.

To find out what Jesus said, and how this story ends, read and consider this scene in John 8:2-11.

Discussion Questions

1. How did the scribes and Pharisees treat this woman?

2. What guilty party was strangely missing from this scene?

3. What emotions did this woman probably experience during this dramatic encounter?

4. Why did the scribes and Pharisees leave when Jesus said, "If any one of you is without sin, let him be the first to throw a stone at her"? (John 8:7-9).

5. Why do you think she stayed, even after her accusers had gone? Why didn't she just slip off when the crowd left?

6. Who is the one who had the right to accuse her? (John 8:46-47).

7. How would you describe the way Jesus treated this woman?

8. What motivated Jesus to forgive her? (John 3:16-17).

9. Since all those in the crowd were confronted with their sin, why was this woman the only one Jesus forgave?

10. Think about Christ's final words to her. How was this woman's new life to be different from her life before?

Considering Christ

As this scene closes, the spotlight lingers on the two key figures: Jesus and the woman who was caught in adultery. Her sin, committed in private, was made public by men not a whit more righteous than she. Yet here she stood—forgiven, protected, and secure in the presence of the only one who could have justly condemned her. Ironically, she was able to take *refuge* in Christ only because her dark, hidden secrets had been exposed . . . and forgiven.

We all long for a similar sense of safety and security. But to experience that kind of spiritual refuge, we, too, must be willing to look honestly at ourselves and to turn from our sin. When the Bible uses the word "sin," it is speaking of the basic tendency we each have to go our own way, to do our own thing.

If the secrets of our hearts were laid open and bare before a holy God, what would He see? What would we see? In the book of Romans, there is a short passage that summarizes the predicament we find ourselves in apart from God's intervention. Read Romans 3:10-12 and try putting these verses in your own words.

There is, thankfully, a more hopeful note following only a few chapters later. In Romans 5:8, what is that message of hope?

God, the heavenly parent, is love, and therefore He wants children upon whom He can lavish His love and receive their love in return.
E. Stanley Jones

[Jesus] loves us and has freed us from our sins by his blood.
Revelation 1:5

4

The Woman Who Worshiped

Jesus Christ is so often pictured in the midst of crowds of people that we sometimes forget that He knew the pleasure of a quiet, intimate evening with close friends.

Mary and Martha and their brother, Lazarus, were some of those who knew the joy of His private company. They often entertained Jesus in their home. Martha orchestrated the dinner while Mary listened attentively to Jesus. In Christ's willingness to teach Mary, He defied the Jewish tradition that held that women need not be taught—indeed, they weren't capable of learning (Luke 10:38-42). Mary was drawn to this man who treated her with such respect. She was accepted and secure in His company.

In this scene, we find Jesus once again having dinner with Mary, Martha, and Lazarus—but this time in the home of Simon the leper. Christ had stopped in Bethany on His way to the great Jewish feast in Jerusalem, the Passover.

Jesus knew that this would be His final trip to Jerusalem. The opposition to His ministry was building. Yet strangely, His closest friends seemed oblivious to the confrontation sure to come—all of His friends, that is, except Mary.

Mary saw the significance of what was happening. This was not merely another pleasant evening spent with Jesus. Mary demonstrated her awareness of the events about to unfold, as well as her devotion to Jesus, by one extraordinary act.

Mary had good reason to express her gratitude to Jesus. At an earlier point, her brother Lazarus had become ill. She and her sister, Martha, sent for Christ, but by the time Jesus got there, Lazarus had been dead for four days. In a moving account in John's Gospel, Jesus raised Lazarus from the dead (John 11:1-44).

To see what Mary did, read Mark 14:1-9. (This passage speaks of an anonymous woman who, we learn from John's account of the same occasion, John 12:1-8, was Mary of Bethany.)

Discussion Questions

1. How would you describe the type of relationship Jesus had with Mary? (John 11:5).

2. What event was Mary thinking about as she anointed Him with this expensive perfume?

3. How much could Mary have sold the perfume for if she had lived today?

4. How did the men around Mary respond to what she did?

How did Jesus respond?

5. What did Mary's action show about her devotion to the Lord Jesus?

Considering Christ
This scene foreshadows the crucifixion of Christ, which is the ultimate statement in all of God's communication with us. God, at last, became the Word that He spoke; that is, He took on human form and lived among us. And now we see Him on His way to being crucified in Jerusalem.

But what does His death really mean? What difference can it make to us as individuals? The Old Testament prophets spoke of the death of the Messiah, Jesus spoke of His own death, and later books in the New Testament explain even further its significance.

Consider these three major references as you seek to formulate your own conclusions about the crucifixion of Jesus Christ.

Isaiah 53:4-6

John 10:14-18

Colossians 2:13-14

God demonstrates his own love for us in this: While
we were still sinners, Christ died for us.

Romans 5:8

5

The Fulfilled Woman

As Christ continued His public ministry, more and more
people began to travel with Him from one town to the
next. Some were no doubt just curious onlookers. But
others followed because they could not help but accompany the person who had so radically changed their lives.
Mary Magdalene was among that latter group. She had
long ago moved from the ranks of the curious to the
convinced.

Little is known of her life before she met Christ
except for this descriptive phrase that occasionally fol-
lows her name: "Mary Magdalene, out of whom [Jesus]
had driven seven demons" (Mark 16:9). Christ healed
her of whatever debilitating physical, emotional, or
spiritual problems engulfed her. She may have been an
obscene screamer, or one who laughed uncontrollably.
Mary was, no doubt, an embarrassment to her family,
avoided in the neighborhood, and restricted from Temple
worship.

But whatever the exact malady of her past, Christ
had given her a new life. She was so grateful that she
joined the group of women who traveled with Christ and
contributed to His support out of their private means. In
fact, the Gospels lead us to conclude, by the prominent
mention of her name, that Mary Magdalene was a leader
among those women.

No heroic acts were ascribed to Mary Magdalene,
but she was present and available to serve Jesus in any
way she could. During the last events of Christ's life and
death, she was an ever-present figure. She was most
likely in the crowd of disciples and friends who accom-
panied Christ on His triumphal entry into Jerusalem.

The group of Jesus' closest followers had all traveled together the sixty or seventy miles on foot from Galilee. And yet, unlike many of Jesus' disciples, Mary remained faithful even when the tide turned against Jesus. She had been with Him when the crowds cheered. She would also be there in His suffering and death.

In all probability, Mary watched Jesus drag the heavy cross to Golgotha. She witnessed the soldiers nail His hands and feet to the cross, and listened to people hurl insults at Him. She felt the earth tremble as darkness filled the sky at three o'clock in the afternoon, and later heard Jesus cry out, "My God, my God, why have you forsaken me?" She stayed near the cross until He died, and then she followed His body to the tomb. (Read Mark 15:33-47 for more details.)

As soon as the Sabbath was over, Mary visited Jesus' grave again. It was almost sunrise, and she brought spices to anoint His body. When she reached the tomb, she was surprised to see that it was open. Mary was privileged to be the first witness of an extraordinary event.

Read about the rest of this event in John 20:10-18.

Discussion Questions

1. What range of emotions must Mary have felt as she endured through the last week of Christ's life?

2. What was Mary Magdalene's initial response to the empty tomb? (John 20:1-2, 11).

3. Why do you think she didn't recognize Jesus?

4. What did Jesus tell her to do? (verse 17).

5. Why do you think Mary was the one He appeared to first after He was raised from the dead?

6. Why is the resurrection of Christ essential to our faith?

Considering Christ
Christ revealed Himself to many people after His resurrection. The end of each Gospel contains a more detailed account of those incidents. A clear summary of those appearances is also found in 1 Corinthians 15:3-8.

The apostle Paul uses this as powerful evidence of the authenticity of Christ and His message. In fact, Paul rather boldly declares the resurrection of Jesus Christ to be the pivotal point of Christianity.

Read 1 Corinthians 15:12-19. Why does Paul say that Jesus' resurrection is so important?

Never before has the world clamored so loudly for answers and never before has it been so committed to the idea that no answers are available.

Ayn Rand

"I am the way and the truth and the life. No one comes to the Father except through me."

Jesus Christ

Wrapping Up Your Study

As these five scenes demonstrate (and the rest of the New Testament bears witness), Jesus treated women as individuals of unique worth and value. Because of His example and model, wherever Christianity has influenced a culture throughout the centuries, the status of women has dramatically changed for the better. No conqueror or religious leader before or since has done for women what Jesus has done.

Yet each of the women in these stories experienced more than the personable, warm response of a compassionate man. The Lord Jesus Christ quite literally transformed the lives of the women in these New Testament accounts.

Jesus longs to meet the needs of women in our generation as well. He is the same yesterday, today, and forever (Hebrews 13:8). You can encounter Christ, just as these women did, by responding to what He has done for you.

Accepting the reality of what Christ has done for you by His death on the Cross is very similar to accepting a gift that another person has purchased for you. That gift is a mark of that person's graciousness toward you—the expression of his or her love.

When you and I accept the gift of God's love in Christ, we are saying that we believe that our sin has created such an insurmountable barrier between us and God that only the death of His Son, Jesus Christ, could bring us back into a right relationship with Him. The following two verses express in a succinct, clear way what that belief really means. How would you put these verses in your own words?

John 1:12

John 5:24

If you would like to begin a new life with Christ, you can express that desire to God very simply in prayer. You can do that by praying and acknowledging to God that you realize you've sinned and you need His forgiveness. You can ask Christ to come into your life right now and give you a new life in Him.

Have you ever taken this step with Jesus Christ?

Do you have any questions about what it means to receive Christ?

Be sure to check out Helene Ashker's other Bible study from NavPress.

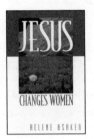

Jesus Changes Women
ISBN: 978-1-57683-077-2

If you want your faith to grow, this study guide will help you learn what it means to become more like Christ as you study elements of spiritual growth.

To order copies, call NavPress at 1-800-366-7788 or log on to www.navpress.com.